HOW TO M...
LAW FIRM ONLINE
INTERNET MARKETING GUIDE

*The #1 Guide for Lawyers and Law Firms
Who Are Ready to Attract More Clients and
Make More Money!"*

HowToMarketYourLawFirmOnline.com

TABLE OF CONTENTS

INTRODUCTION

Thank you for reading our Internet marketing & Search Engine Optimization (SEO) Guide for Lawyers and Law Firms.

In this guide we will walk you step-by-step through the process of marketing your law firm online by optimizing your website from an SEO perspective and explain:

- How the search engines work (PPC vs. map listings vs. organic) and what you need to do to handle each for maximum return.

- How to build authority online & how to use an authority building strategy so that your law firm ranks above the competition.

- Our search engine optimization strategy for law firms.

- The importance of law firm keywords. This single insight is invaluable for you as a lawyer.

- The most important online directories that you MUST be listed on.

- Our social media strategy specifically for the law firm industry.

- The Marketing Sales Funnel every law firm should be using and much more.

WHY SEO IS SO IMPORTANT FOR LAWYERS & LAW FIRMS

Most lawyers already understand that the Internet & search engines are EXTREMELY important to the long term growth and sustainability of their business but occasionally I get the question "Why are search engines and search engine marketing so important to the law firm Industry?"

Yellow Pages Are No Longer Effective

It used to be that the #1 place clients looked when they needed a lawyer was the Yellow Pages. In today's market, very few people still reference the printed Yellow Pages. In fact the new generation has not even been exposed to the Yellow Pages and only know the Internet as a way to search for local businesses.

Where do people search now?

They look on the search engines (Google, Yahoo, Bing & others) and social media sites (LinkedIn, Facebook, Twitter) or ask for referrals from friends and family.

- A new survey of 2,000 consumers found that 86 percent of those surveyed used the Internet to find a local business.

- 74 percent of the respondents said they use a search engine when they are looking for a local retail or service business.

If you're not showing up on page one of Google, Yahoo & Bing for the law firm related keywords in your area, then you are missing a major opportunity! In this guide we will show you how you can ensure that you put your best foot forward and show up in as many local lawyer related searches in your city and practice as possible.

UNDERSTANDING HOW THE SEARCH ENGINES WORK

O ver the past ten years the way the search engines work has changed significantly; especially with the introduction of the Google map listings (Google Plus Local) to the search results for local search. A majority of the lawyers we talk with are confused about how the search engines work and the differences between the map listings, organic listings & the paid / Pay-Per-Click listings.

In this section we wanted to take a few minutes to DEMYSTIFY the search engines and break down the anatomy of the search engine results page (SERPs). By understanding how each component works, you can formulate a strategy to maximize the results of each.

There are 3 core components of the search engines results page:

1. Paid / PPC Listings

2. Map Listings

3. Organic Listings

Paid / PPC Listings

In the paid section of the search engines you are able to select the keywords that are relevant to you and then pay to be listed in this area. The reason it is referred to PPC or Pay-Per-Click is because rather than paying a flat monthly or daily fee for placement, you simply pay each time someone clicks on the link. The PPC platform is based on a bidding system and the company that bids the highest gets the best placement. PPC is still a good way to market your business online, but should be thought of as a short term marketing solution. PPC can get very expensive very fast, with some keywords costing as much as $30.00 per click in the law firm industry.

Map Listings

The map listings have become very important because it is the first thing that comes up in the search results for most locally based searches. If someone searches "lawyer + your city" chances are the map listings will be the first thing they look at. Unlike the paid section of the search engine, you can't buy your way into the map listings you have to earn it, and once you do, there is no per click cost associated with being in this section of the search engine.

Organic Listings

The organic / natural section of the search engine results page appears directly beneath the map listings in many local searches, but appears directly beneath the paid listings in the absence of the map listings (the map section only shows up in specific local searches). Similar to the map listings, you can't pay your way into this section of the search engines and there is no per click cost associated with it.

Now that you understand the 3 major components of the search engine results and the differences between paid listings, map listings & organic listings you might wonder… "What section is most important?" This is a question that we receive from lawyers every day.

The fact is that all three components are important and each should have a place in your online marketing program because you want to show up as often as possible when someone is searching for your services in your practice area. With that said, assuming you are operating on a limited budget and need to make each marketing dollar count; you need to focus your investment on the sections that are going to drive the strongest return on investment.

Research indicates that a vast majority of the population look directly at the organic & map listings when searching and their eyes simply glance over the paid listings.

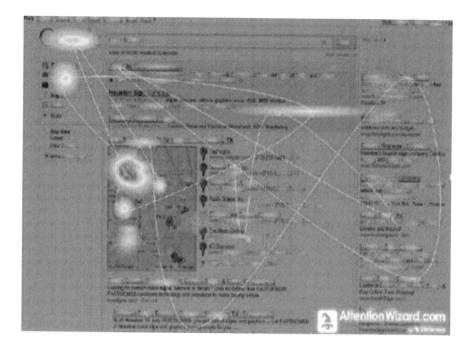

This heat map indicates where the searcher tends to view as they come onto a search engine results page.

Where People Click on the Google

Search Engine Results Pages

So if you are operating on a limited budget and need to get the best bang for your buck, you should start by focusing your efforts on the area that gets the most clicks at the lowest cost. We have found that placement in the organic and map section on the search engines drive a SIGNIFICANTLY better return on investment than Pay-Per-Click marketing.

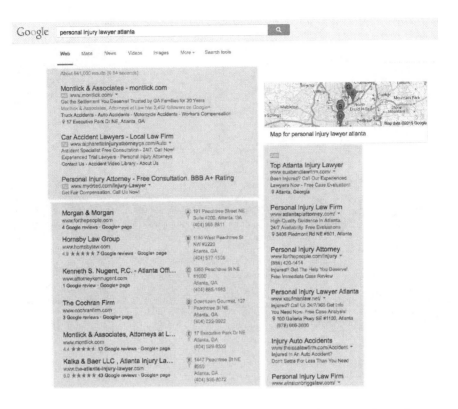

So what can do to get your law firm listed in the organic and map listings? That is what we are going to be covering in the following chapters in the guide.

72%
OF THE CLICKS

28%
OF THE CLICKS

Organic and Map Listings

These results are not paid for; they're the product of Google's crawling the web and processing what it finds.

Pay Per Click Areas

These results have been paid for by advertisers through Google's Adwords program.

GETTING YOUR LAW FIRM ON THE GOOGLE MAPS

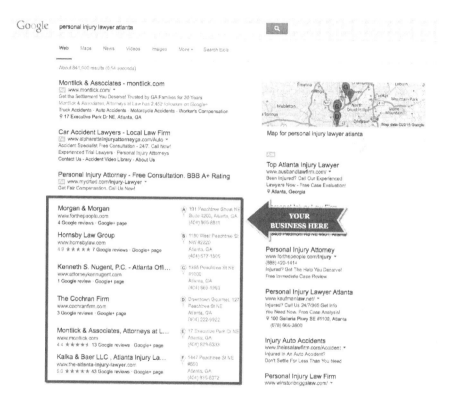

If you are just getting started in Internet marketing for your law firm and are just trying to get an idea of how to get your firm listed on the Google Map, this is a great place to start. I am going to cover the core fundamentals of what the Google Map is, how it works, and what you need to do to at least get the ball rolling in the right direction towards getting you placed on the map.

Fundamentally the Google Map or Google+ Local listing is what shows up when you type in your city plus your practice area on Google. Up along the top, and along the side is the pay per click, and in the center at the very top of the results page is typically the map listings or what we call Google Places or the Google Map listings. Directly below that in local search is what are typically the organic listings. There is a lot of information about search engine optimization, meta tags, meta descriptions and all of the like but really this is a totally different realm of search engine optimization known as Google Places Optimization.

So, what do you need to do in order to make sure that you are listed on that map, and more importantly make sure you are showing up on page one over time? There are a number of things you can do, and there are multiple layers of complexity, strategies and things that you can do. The most important thing you can do from the starting point perspective is to go to http://www.Google.com/MyBusiness.

Google has set up this website for business owners to tangibly claim their Google Places listing. If you go there you are going to see two different buttons. On the left side you are going to see one that says, "Consumer / Write Reviews." On the right side it says "Business Owner? Get Started." Obviously you want to click on the one that says, "Business owner? Get Started," and what that will do is take you through the process of claiming your Google Places listing.

The latest statistics indicate that more than 89 percent of users or businesses haven't claimed their Google Places listing. This creates a great opportunity for your to beat your competition to the punch. One of the first things you want to do is go to http://Google.com/Places.com

and claim your listing so you can at least make sure it's got all of your right information. Your phone number, your website address (if you have one) description of what you do, some pictures and testimonials. More than anything else make sure that you have control of your own business listing on Google.com, in the places listings.

Some things to be aware of as you claim your Google Places listing. The process is relatively simple. If you have got a Gmail account or some type of Google account, Google will recognize that and let you use that to claim your Google Places listing. If you don't, you're going to need to go through the process of establishing your Google account. So that you can claim your Google Places listing.

Once you have logged in, you will need to type in your phone number and firm name. Then, the system will search the Google Places directory to see if you already exist in the database. In most cases if you have been in business for any period of time for more than a year, you're typically going to show up on the list already. So Google will pull up your existing listing and ask you to confirm it's your and claim your listing. If you don't, there is another process that will let you add yourself to Google Places. So if you're a new business or if for some reason you don't already exist in the Google Places directory, you would press "add new listing."

In either event it's going to walk you step by step through the process. You're going to type in your firm name, address, and phone number. You're going to make sure all of that information is correct. A couple of things to pay attention to as you do that.

Make sure that you use your actual firm name. So if you're, "Smith Law Group LLP," make sure that you name it, "Smith Law Group LLP," and not some other facsimile thereof like "Traffic Legal Services" or "Smith Law Group, Your Traffic Legal Services Firm." Don't add additional key words in that name. It's against the Google Places rules and policies. Make sure you keep your name, the actual name of your company.

It is important that you establish your NAP (Name, Address, Phone Number Profile) and that it consistently referenced the same way across the web. That it's showing your company name, phone number, and address the same way every time. As a starting point, if you're getting started with Google Places, make sure that you make it very simple. And that you use the same methodology for naming yourself across the board. Same with your address. If you're at 105 SW 10th Street, Suite 105, use that same exact wording. If you're going to use SW use SW. If you're going to spell out Southwest, spell out Southwest. If you're going to use your suite number, "Suite 105". Make sure you either list it, or you don't list it, and decide whether it's going to be "unit number" or "suite number". List it that same way every single time.

Moving on, once you have added the fundamentals, make sure you add your website address. This is very important. If you don't have a website, I definitely recommend getting a website setup. In this guide I share what pages you want to build to your website from an SEO perspective. Suffice it to say, add your website there. It's obviously going to drive links to your website, but it is also going to make it easier for your clients to get to you when they do find you on the map.

In your description, I always encourage trying to make sure you list your practice areas and your geographic market in the description. E.G. "Your company is your Dallas Law Firm Personal Injury Attorney. We provide personal injury representation to victims in Dallas and the surrounding parts of Texas." You have only got about 250 characters for the description so really try and maximize that space to its fullest capability.

Directly below that, you have categories. You want to, obviously, choose the categories that most specifically match what your business does. Don't add yourself to categories that aren't relevant. You can add five categories and use the categories Google suggests. Make sure they are in the order you want, as they will appear in that order. Also, make sure they appear in Google search results for local, as those are relevant categories.

You do have the option to create custom categories. But always exercise the already available categories as much as possible, as opposed to creating some unique category name.

Moving down the list, the next thing that you see is the ability to upload photos and videos. I encourage you, you need to upload as much content here as possible because Google is looking for a complete profile. The more information that you have in there the more complete your profile appears. You can upload up to ten pictures & five videos. Try and use real pictures and not stock photography. Try and upload pictures that are representative of your firm.

Video. You can upload up to five videos, and the videos connect through YouTube. Don't miss out on this opportunity. You should absolutely upload all five videos here. Remember that you are a law firm so although it does not need to be super hi-tech it does need to be professional. Consider hiring a professional to shoot the videos.

The video needs to be representative of who you are and what you do. What we find is, having a video, obviously it's going to help build out your Google Places profile which improves your probability of showing up on the map, because information is power in the Google era.

It's also going to help people resonate with your firm. If they can feel like they get to know, like, and trust you before they have to decide whether they are going to call you or not. It improves the probability of getting that call, and getting that piece of business. So, upload five videos to YouTube and then connect them to your Google Places listing. Ideal scenario: ten pictures, five videos.

The next section is the Service Area. You can select your Practice Area based off your location & miles included in your service area. Try to make this a legitimate representation of your true service area (don't over do it).

The last field on the Google Places listing is additional information. Here you will find basically just two fields. One on the left, one on the right, and it basically lets you type in whatever you want. In a lot of cases, people left to their own devices will get to that section and just press submit, then feel like they're done. This is the area where you can really add a lot of valuable content, a lot of specific information about who you are and what you do, and the specific practice areas that you offer.

Once you have got all of those things filled in. And you feel comfortable that you have got the right images, you have got the right description, you have got the right content listed in the additional information, then, you go to the next step and press "Submit."

This is where the verification process takes place. Google gives you two options for verifying your listing. Depending upon if it's a new listing, sometimes they don't offer the phone verification process. Typically, you have the choice verify via phone, or verify via mail.

I always encourage you, if you do have the option, to verify via phone. Just to go ahead and verify via phone, because it is an instantaneous process. You press verify via phone. You will get a message indicating that Google will be calling that number with your PIN. Whatever your business number is. As soon as you press submit, a call comes into your business line. So make sure you have got someone available to answer that call directly. It will be an automated system that calls with a message like "this is Google, your pin number is 43625" for instance. Then, you type that into your Google Places account online. You have now officially claimed and verified your Google Places listing.

If you don't have that option for whatever reason, and I have seen cases where Google is not making the phone verification process available, then you need to press "Submit" to verify via mail. Then you would receive a post card, via the mail, within typically within three to five business days. It has a pin code just like the other option. It takes a little bit longer this way but at least you get your pin and you are able to log back in and verify your account and be off the ground.

Now once you have verified your Google Places listing, now you have the ability to go in and post status updates and more. I would encourage you to log back into the account. Up on the top right hand corner you will see, "Dashboard" and on the right you will see, "Offers."

Fundamentally, that's where you want to start. You want to go to www. google.com/places, build out your listing as I have described. And now you have got a placeholder and a higher probability of showing up on the Google map. I wish I could tell you it is just as easy as that and you're going to be on Page One for your City + Your Practice. Unfortunately, it's not that simple, because there are hundreds of businesses in your area, if not thousands, all doing the same type of thing. A lot of them have claimed their Google Places listing. So, at this point it really doesn't give you a free pass to the front of the line. But it does get you on the list.

Really, the next step in getting placed on Google Places on the map, is obtaining consistent name, address, citation profile across the web, and getting online reviews from legitimate users. When I say establish, consistent name, address, phone number, profile across the web, we talked about the fact when you claimed your Google Places listing, you wanted to use the same name, address, and phone number across the board.

Now what you want to do is make sure that you have got yourself on other important online directories. Because Google looks across the web and it says, "OK, John the Criminal Law Attorney, in Memphis has a Google Places listing, but where else are they listed online?" They look at a lot of different places. They look at Yahoo Local. They look at Bing Local. They look at Superpages. They look at Avvo. They look at YP.com and the list goes on and on.

They pull data from info providers like InfoUsa and others. So, in order to improve your probability, you need to make sure you're showing up in all of these different places with a consistent name, address, phone number, and profile. That's another thing Google looks at. Just making sure that you're credible, and that you do exist on other online directories.

The other really important thing you need to do, in order to improve the probability of showing up on the map, is to get reviews from real clients online. You will notice that the companies showing up on spots A-F on page one have a tendency to have a large quantity of reviews.

I will point out that you don't want to try and game the system on reviews. It might be easy to think, "I'll just go out there and set up a bunch of accounts and I will write up a bunch of reviews, and I'll have 55 reviews on my account then I should be good to go." It's not that simple. Make sure you have real reviews. Do not create fake reviews – false reviews are a bar violation. The quantity and quality do matter. Also make sure the reviews don't come from the same IP address as your firm. Google seems to track the computer that the review is posted from. Your reviews need to come from different IPs of your own client's computers or mobile devices.

Google does have algorithms in place to prevent people from gaming the system. Really they are looking at the reviewer's profile. In order to write a review on Google Places, you have to have a Gmail, or a Google account. Google knows the historic profile of those that have Google accounts. They watch their search trends. They have IP information which gives them information about where they are located. A lot of cases, they have entered and volunteered that information. "I'm located at this address, and they have frequented these types of web sites." So Google has a pretty good idea who legitimate users of their Google search engine, one of the most frequented sites in existence. They have data on just about everybody. If you're trying to game the system, Google will catch that.

You want to make sure that you have a process within your business to solicit reviews from legitimate people who have used your services. You will want to implement a review acquisition process, a review acquisition system, which includes sending an email out to the people in your sphere of influence, asking them to write a review along with a follow-up system to distribute the review online and through social media platforms.

We also have a few tools that we use for reputation marketing and reviews. One that we have available is through http://birdeye.com/ that gives you the ability to, be found by search engines — accurate and up-to-date — on all the major sites that matter most to your prospective clients. We have found that to be the ultimate strategy for really passing your authentic service area data to Google and getting reviews on a consistent basis. BirdEye aggregates your reviews from all the top sites so you can easily monitor what your clients are saying about you — in real-time! Again that's http://birdeye.com/. We've got a whole series of information on that for our clients. How it works, and why it's valuable.

Again just to cover the fundamentals of what you want to do from a starting point to really get started on Google Places and get the ball rolling in the right direction. First, go to www.google.com/places. Claim your Google Places listings with some of the specifications that I defined earlier.

Then, really get aggressive with your name, address, and profile information across the web. Go onto websites like; CitySearch, Judy's Book, Avvo and YP.com and make sure that you're listed there and that your information is consistent.

Then, launch an aggressive process for getting reviews from authentic clients.

If you start to do these things on a consistent basis you will start to show up on the Google map, in your area when people search "your practice + your city".

HOW TO CLAIM & OPTIMIZE YOUR GOOGLE MAP LISTING

There are a number of best practices that you want to be aware of to properly optimize your Map listing.

- Firm Name – Always use your legal Firm Name – don't stuff additional fields into the Name Field. E.G. So if you're, "Smith Law Group LLP," make sure that you name it, "Smith Law Group LLP," and not some other facsimile thereof like "Traffic Legal Services" or "Smith Law Group, Your Traffic Legal Services Firm." This would be against the Google Places Guidelines and will reduce your probability of ranking.

- Address – On the "Address Field" use your EXACT legal address. Be intentional here. You want to ensure that you have the same address listed on your Google Places listing as it is on all the other online directory listings like YellowPages.com, CitySearch.com, Yelp.com, etc. The consistency of your N.A.P (Name, Address, Phone Number Profile) is very important for placement.

- Phone Number – Use a local (not 800#) and use your real office number rather than a tracking number. We find that 800#'s don't rank well. If you use a tracking number it won't be consistent with your other Online Directory Listings and ultimately won't rank well.

- Categories – You can use up to five categories, so use ALL five. Be sure to use categories that describe what your business "is" rather than what it "does". So you can use "Personal Injury Attorney" "Personal Injury Law Firm" and "Atlanta Personal Injury Law Firm" rather than "Personal Injury Attorney Fighting for Your Rights" or "Attorney on Your Side" the latter would be considered a violation of Google's regulations and would hurt rather than help you.

- Practice Area & Location settings – Google offers 2 options here 1. No, All clients come to my location 2. Yes, I serve clients at their location. As a law firm you need to select "No, All clients come to my location" because clearly your clients are visiting your location. Not doing so can result in a penalty on your listing.

- The next option once you click "No, All clients come to my location" is "Show my address". If you happen to work from a Home Office it is required that you select "Do not show my address" not doing so put's you at risk of having your listing deleted.

- If you don't have a Business Address or a Home Address to list the only other option is a Virtual Office. Unfortunately P.O. Box Addresses & Mail Boxes Etc. Addresses don't tend to rank well.

- Picture & Video Settings – You can upload up to 10 pictures & 5 videos. Use this opportunity to upload authentic content about your company. It's always best to use real photos of your firm and team rather than Stock Photos.

- Pictures – Be sure to invest in professional pictures. You can also create geo context for the photos by uploading them to a video sharing site like Panoramio.com (a Google Property) that enables you to Geo Tag your photo's to your company location.

- Videos – Upload VIDEOS. Remember that you are a law firm so although it does not need to be super hi-tech it does need to be professional. Consider hiring a professional to shoot the videos. A best practice is to upload the video's to YouTube and then Geo Tag them using advanced settings.

Once you have Optimized your listing using the best practices referenced above, you want to be sure that you don't have any duplicate listings listed on Google Maps. We have found that even just one or two duplicate listings can prevent your listing from ranking on page one. In order to identify and merge duplicate listings run a search on Google for "Company Name, City".

To clean up duplicate listings, click on the listing in question and then click "edit business details"

- Then click "This is a duplicate" and let Google Know that the listing should be merged with your primary listing.

If you follow these best practices you will have a well optimized Google Maps listing for your Law Firm. The next step is to Establish your NAP (Name, Address, Phone Number Profile) Across the web.

GOOGLE MAP
OPTIMIZATION TIPS

Now that you have claimed your Local Business Listing on Google, Yahoo & Bing you need to take additional steps to improve your placement on the maps in your area.

- Establish a Consistent NAP– You need to establish a consistent NAP (Name Address & Phone Number) across the Internet, on your website, as well as on the major Data Providers (InfoUSA, Super Pages, Yelp, City Search, etc).

- Consistent Name – Pick the format for your name & stick with it e.g. "Smith Law Group LLP" not "Traffic Legal Services".

- Consistent Address – If your address is 1267 SW 29 St, Suite 10 you want to be sure that it reads that exact way and not 1267 SW 29 St #10.

- Consistent Phone Number – You want to use the same number on each of these sites (if you don't, it will hurt you).

- Use a LOCAL not a Toll Free Phone Number.

- Get Reviews – Reviews are a key determinant of placement within the Map Listings.

- The number of reviews of your local listing is a key determinant in placement.

- As a practice, you need to request reviews from your clients in order to get them.

- Build out your Places Page – You have the option to upload photos, videos and coupons.

- Fill your Places page with quality content. Add all 10 photos your office, staff, company logo, etc.

- Upload a video or two. Remember that you are a law firm so although it does not need to be super hi-tech it does need to be professional. Consider hiring a professional to shoot the videos. A best practice is to upload the video's to YouTube and then Geo Tag them using advanced settings. Record yourself explaining who the company is, what you do, and what your unique selling proposition is.

- Select the Right Categories – You have the option to choose up to 5 categories. It is very important to select the appropriate categories and/or add new custom categories, as needed.

- Increase your Citations – All things being equal, citations are a key determinant of placement. Just like in SEO where inbound links determine placement with local listings, citations determine placement. He who has the most quality citations wins.

- Citations are listings across the web that contain your NAP (Name Address & Phone Number) with or without a link.

In order to build up your citations:

- Add yourself to the local directory sites where you are not currently listed.

- InfoUsa

- Yelp

- City Search

- Super Pages

- Insider Pages

- Search for "your industry, directory"

- Search "your city, directory"

- Look at the listings of the people who have spot A, B & C on the Map for your services and look that their citations. In many cases you can go out and get those same citations!

SEO STRATEGY FOR LAWYERS AND LAW FIRMS

S EO, or Search Engine Optimization, is the process of getting your website to show up in the Organic (FREE / Non-PPC) section of the search engines. There are specific things that you can do both on and off your website to ensure that you show up when someone types "Lawyers + Your City" into Google, Yahoo or Bing.

Step 1 – Build out your website & obtain more place holders on the major search engines.

A typical law firm site has only 5-6 pages (Home – Practice Areas – Attorney Profiles - FAQs - Contact Us). That does not create a lot of indexation or place holders on the major search engines. Most lawyers and law firms practice in more than one area including bankruptcy, divorce, DUI, criminal law, traffic, business law, intellectual property, etc. just to name a few. By BUILDING out the website and creating separate pages for each of these practice areas (combined with city modifiers), you can get listed on the search engines for each of those different keyword combinations. Here is an example:

- Home – About Us– Practice Area – Contact Us

- Sub Pages for Each Practice – Atlanta Bankruptcy Lawyer, Atlanta Bankruptcy Law Lawyer, Atlanta Lawyer, Atlanta Bankruptcy, Free Consultation Atlanta , Bankruptcy Lawyer, etc.

Step 2 – Optimize Pages for Search Engines:

Once the pages are built for each of your core practice area and sub-pages, each of the pages need to be Optimized from an SEO perspective so that the search engines understand what the page is about and list you for those words. Here are some of the most important items that need to be taken care of for on-page search engine optimization:

- Unique Title Tag on each page
- H1 Tag re-stating that Title Tag on each Page
- Images named with primary keywords
- URL should contain page keyword
- Anchor Text on each page and built into footer – Atlanta lawyer
- XML Sitemap should be created & submitted to Google Webmaster Tools and

Bing Webmaster Tools

Typical Lawyer Website Title Tag:

- Personal Injury Law Firm

VS.

SEO Optimized Title Tag:

- Charlotte Lawyer | Personal Injury Lawyer | Lawyer In NC

If you do just one thing today to start optimizing your website, make sure you work on your title tags. Make sure that you DO NOT use the same title tag on each page.

Step 3 – Inbound Links

Once the pages are built out and the "on-page" SEO is complete, the next step is getting inbound links. Everything we have done to this point is laying the ground work – you have to have the pages in order to even be in the running...but it is the number of QUALITY inbound links to those pages that is going to determine placement.

So once the pages are built out we are really just getting started. The only way to get your site to rank above your competition is by having MORE quality inbound links to your site. There are a number of things that you can do to increase the number of inbound links to your site.

- Association Links – Be sure that you have a link to your site from any industry associations that you belong to Lawyer associations, Chamber of Commerce, Networking Groups, etc.

- Directory Listings – Get your site listed on as many authoritative directory type listings as possible

- Create Interesting Content / Articles about your industry - this is probably the #1 source of inbound links because you can write an article about "What to expect when hiring a lawyer" and push it out to thousands of article directory sites, each containing a link back to a specific page on your site.

If you build out your site for your services and sub-services, optimize the pages using SEO best practices and then systematically obtain inbound links to those pages and sub-pages, you will start to DOMINATE the search engines for the lawyer related keywords in your area. We provide 10 additional link building strategies later in the guide.

In order to help you determine what pages should be built out for your site, we have researched the most commonly searched lawyer related keywords. By knowing these keywords and implementing them into your updated website, you can ensure that you don't miss out on valuable traffic to your site. On the next page is our list of the most commonly searched lawyer keywords.

LAWYER KEYWORDS

One of the most important components of Search Engine Optimization is Keyword Research. You need to know what people are actually searching for so that you can optimize your site for keywords that will actually drive valuable traffic.

It is important to keep in mind that a legal website will not just appear on page 1 of Google or in the top searches without correct search engine optimization. It is also important to rank for long tail keywords in addition to short tail keywords.

Based on our research (reviewing the historic trends on Google, Yahoo & Bing) we suggest that you develop a list of the most commonly searched keywords for the law firm industry + your city + your practice area. Use these long keywords on your website, in your blog posts, on social media posts and in your videos.

There are free and paid keyword search tools and we listed a few tools below:

- Ubersuggest
- KeywordSpy
- SEMRush
- SpyFu
- WordTracker
- Majestic SEO

DIRECTORY MARKETING FOR LAWYERS AND LAW FIRMS

Ten years ago, you could place a BIG ad in the Yellow Pages and connect with a large percentage of your local clients when they were in need of your services.

Today, people go to a number of places including Google, Yahoo & Bing, but they also go to online directories. Below are the most important and searched directories that you want to make sure that you are listed in:

- Google Places
- Yahoo Local
- Bing Local
- Avvo
- YP.com
- Superpages

You can add your company to most of these directly FREE of charge and that will serve its purposes from a citation development perspective (getting your name, address and phone number more visible online, but don't count on these free listings to drive a lot of call volume or traffic.)

Although these directories aren't free we have seen them drive a solid return on investment:

- Martindale.com

- Lawyers.com

- Findlaw.com

- AngiesList.com

- Local.botw.org

- Judysbook.com

We have also included a directory list of some of the best free law firm directories we have found online in the guide.

Law Firm Directory List:

Alphalegal	http://www.alphalegal.com/
Attorney Directorydb	http://attorneydirectorydb.org/
AttorneyFee	http://attorneyfee.com/
AttorneysLawyers	http://www.attorneyslawyers.org/
AttorneyYellowPages	http://attorneyyellowpages.com/
Avvo	http://www.avvo.com/free-lawyer-advertising
Best Attorneys Online	http://www.bestattorneysonline.com/
CourthouseSquare.com	http://www.courthousesquare.com/become-a-member/index/type/professional/member-type/company
Dilawctory	http://www.dilawctory.com/
eLocal Lawyer	http://www.elocallawyers.com/

Law Firm Directory List:

Find Lawyer by City	http://www.findlawyersbycity.com/
FindLaw	http://flcas.findlaw.com/auth.jsp?tk=HtEy ccWTNSOKiLRgB9A8JZ04NtGxdj5s&a pp=3041
FindMeALawyer	http://www.findmealawyer.com/
HG.org	http://www.hg.org/
Justia	http://lawyers.justia.com/new-profile
Law Fuel	http://www.lawfuel.com/directory/ membership-account/
Law Referral	http://lawreferralconnect.com/
LawBlogs	http://www.lawblogs.net/content/ participate-lawblogs
LawDeeDa	https://www.lawdeeda.com
LawFirmDirectory	http://lawfirmdirectory.org/
LawGuru	http://lawguru.com/answers/atty_profile/ apply/
LawLink	http://lawlink.com/
LawQA	http://www.lawqa.com/
Lawyer Legion	http://lawyers.lawyerlegion.com/create. php
Lawyer Ratingz	http://www.lawyerratingz.com/
Lawyercentral	http://www.lawyercentral.com/claim-my-attorney-profile.html
LawyersDB	http://www.lawyersdb.com/register.php
Lead Counsel	http://www.leadcounsel.org/
Legal Docs	http://www.legaldocs.com/
Legal Financing	http://www.legalfeefinancing.org/

Law Firm Directory List:

LegalWebFinder	http://www.legalwebfinder.com/
List-Lawyers	http://www.list-lawyers.com/
MoreLaw	https://secure.morelaw.com/add/attorney/
My Legal Practice	http://www.mylegalpractice.com/
PathLegal	http://pathlegal.com/register/lawyer_profile.php
Target Law	http://targetlaw.com/
USA Attorneys	http://usaattorneys.org/
USLegal	http://lawyers.uslegal.com/
Wholly Legal	http://whollylegal.com/

SOCIAL MEDIA STRATEGIES FOR LAW FIRMS

There is a lot of BUZZ around Social Media (Facebook, Twitter, YouTube), but how can Social Media be leveraged by a lawyer? How can you actually use social media to grow your law firm?

It all starts with understanding that Social Media is the new word of mouth. The best way to use Social Media is to enhance the engagement / loyalty of your existing clients and by extension of that and social media platforms, you will grow your repeat business and word of mouth business.

Setup and optimize your social media profiles on the major social sites for your company:

- Facebook

- Twitter

- YouTube

- LinkedIn

- SlideShare

- YouTube

- Send an email blast to your existing email list (if you have one) letting them know that you want to connect with them on social media & that you now have social profiles. Ask them to "Like You", "Follow You" and / or "subscribe" to you.

- Add social media to your day-to-day business practices and systematically invite your clients to engage with you online.

- Add links to your business cards, brochures, marketing materials, website and email signature

- Be sure to invite all of your clients to engage with you online

- POST VALUABLE CONTENT – This may be the most important component of your   Social Media Strategy. If you have thousands of fans and followers, but don't add value…you will have accomplished nothing. You need to post relevant updates, tips, ideas, techniques, news and calls to actions on a daily basis. Try to keep 90% of your posts informational & 10% (or less) promotional.

- Engage with your clients – You need to stay on top of your social media profiles and engage with your fans / followers when / if they post or reply to your profiles.

- Be sure to abide by the Rules of Professional Conduct for your state and make sure that if you hire an online marketing agency that they are aware of these guidelines and part of an organization dedicated to the advancement of legal marketing and business development professionals.

VIDEO MARKETING STRATEGIES FOR LAW FIRMS

If you're on the first page of Google search results for "things you want to be known for," you win. If you're on page 2, you might as well be on page 200; you lose. This is a brutal competition, and you're up against the same lawyers here as you are in your practice: same competition, different battlefield.

In order to be found on the Web, you need to put information there that your prospective clients will find. That information has to be relevant and useful, and it needs to be distinctive and representative about your firm.

You likely have been told that videos can improve your Internet marketing results; but how?

Have you ever considered answering legal questions on video? What about posting the videos on your website, social media sites and ? That's providing real value. That's a real differentiator from your competition— building authority and engaging with your prospective clients online through video.

How to Build Your Law Firm Video Marketing Strategy:

Create a video marketing plan: We recommend creating a strategy and creating videos that position you as the trusted authority and expert.

Be consistent: We recommend publishing one new video per week on a topic that helps build trust, authority and expert status in your practice area.

Keep videos short: Search online for topics and keywords before creating videos. Keep video topics from 1 to 3 minutes.

Syndicate the videos: Share the videos through social networks, blogs, YouTube and sites like SoundCloud.

Maximize video recording sessions: We recommend creating a strategy and recording multiple videos during one session. If possible record 10-20 videos and have your editor distribute 1 video per week.

Measure results. Create a call to action use a trackable number, track engagement and measure results. Video is a form of communication, builds trust and can be used to build authority online when used strategically.

Quick tip: Answer common from AskaLawyer.com. All of the questions from this site come from real people and many of the questions could be like those from your prospective clients. Be sure to pick the general topics. Example Strategy: "5 Things You Need to Know Before Hiring a ____ Lawyer"

YOUR LAWYER AND LAW FIRM MARKETING SALES FUNNEL

Effective marketing leads to an end result. We created a marketing sales funnel that demonstrates how we help our clients attract, connect, engage and inspire prospect to take action.

Your marketing plan must have a strategic goal to produce results that inspire your clients to take action. We do this with a 26 or 52 week outlined content marketing plan for each of our clients. Our goal is to help our clients ACE - IT!

Use the marketing sales funnel below as you create your marketing plan so that you ACE - IT with your marketing plan online!

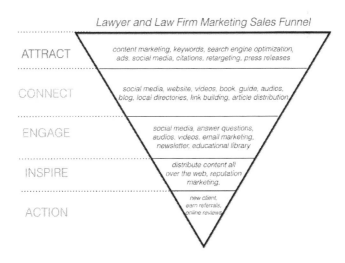

Lawyer and Law Firm Marketing Sales Funnel

ATTRACT — content marketing, keywords, search engine optimization, ads, social media, citations, retargeting, press releases

CONNECT — social media, website, videos, book, guide, audios, blog, local directories, link building, article distribution

ENGAGE — social media, answer questions, audios, videos, email marketing, newsletter, educational library

INSPIRE — distribute content all over the web, reputation marketing.

ACTION — new client, earn referrals, online reviews

10 LINK BUILDING STRATEGIES FOR LAW FIRMS

L ink building is absolutely critical to increase your search ranking on Google. Online marketing and ranking involves much more than a website. You must also include additional strategies that build your authoritative status online and position you as the expert.

What is Link building?

When one website links to another website, it's called a link. Other terms used commonly by SEO companies and online marketers include: backlink, linkback, inbound link, incoming link, inlinks, and inward links. Links to your site are important for because search engines use them as a gauge of a website's relevance and authority.

How to I build high quality links back to my website?

The best way to acquire "good" backlinks, inbound links, is to create unique, relevant content that helps your prospective clients. If you're a personal injury attorney in Atlanta, this might mean creating a "Myths About Personal Injury Cases" to educate clients. If you're a bankruptcy attorney in Charlotte, you might create a "Can I File Bankruptcy Without a Lawyer?" article, video or audio that answers this question and post it on YouTube, Findlaw.com or Clarity.FM. There are quite a few attorneys on this site https://clarity.fm/browse/search/lawyer.

Here's a list of 10 ways to get inbound links for your website:

1. Chamber of Commerce

When you join a chamber of commerce, you automatically get added to their online business directory under your business category. Google values these trusted links to your website when calculating search rankings. Be sure to fully optimize your listing.

2. Better Business Bureau

The Better Business Bureau is an established form of social proof and trust to consumers all over the United States. On the web, trust and authority are important when it comes to search rankings. Getting a link from BBB.org is one of the best inbound links a lawyer can have leading to their website.

3. Publish Press Releases and Industry Updates and Changes

Releasing online Press Releases using services such as PRWeb, PRlog, or Marketwired can put information about your business in the hands of journalists who can distribute the content all over the web. A recent submission was made for Family Law Attorney Mark Baer Named to Top One Percent List by The National Association of Distinguished Counsel and this builds authority and credibility online. Using this strategy you can can include links back to your site so you could earn thousands of inbound links if these online press releases get distributed well. We also recommend including industry changes and updates in your local business chronicles and alumni sites as well.

4. Legal Trade Associations and Magazines

Make sure your website is listed in the members' directories of any trade associations you belong to. When you are featured in an online magazine be sure to comment on the article if possible online with a backlink to your site. This will help maximize your online visibility and drive new leads, promote your achievements to potential clients.

5. Answer Questions

When the opportunity comes along to answer questions create videos or audio responses. You can post the video on your social media site with a backlink to your website.

6. Join a charity.

Being a part of charity board is great for building authority so be sure that there is a backlink to your site.

7. Interviews

Interviews are a great way to gain links back to your site. Sign up for HARO - Help A Reporter Out to locate opportunities. www.haro.com and http://www.radioguestlist.com the #1 free radio guest, podcast, and talk show guest expert interview booking service.

8. Submit your company for awards

This is a great way to get a link back to your site, recognition as one of the best law firms . Best of all it's free. http://bestlawfirms.usnews.com/faq.aspx

9. Book a segment on the local news

A powerful way to get backlinks is by doing a local news segment that is featured on Fox News, ABC, NBC or CBS and posted on their website. We have regular segments on CBS in Charlotte, NC and help our clients get booked on segments too.

10. Volunteer at a local school

.edu links are golden. Many schools and universities will link back to your site. Just check to be sure.

TIMES HAVE CHANGED

Has your law firm changed with it?

Looking at the infographic, below, you can see the old forms of media are really no longer the top places to market your business. Gone are the Yellow Pages, direct mail, signage, $10k billboards and $1800 per month 30 second commercials. Those forms of media are still very expensive and give little ROI.

The top forms of media are now the Internet, SMS and audio/video podcasting. By reading this guide you are well on your way in the right direction.

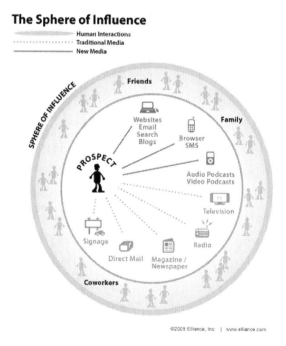

The Sphere of Influence

Human Interactions
Traditional Media
New Media

©2009 Elliance, Inc | www.elliance.com

YOUR COMPLETE WEBSITE CHECKLIST

We created this checklist to provide you with ideas for getting your website ready for the search engines.

Domain name & URLs

Why this is important: The domain name is part of the identity of your business. The URL chosen can have a significant impact on brand identity and in a lesser extent, keyword ranking performance. However, how your site domain name and page URLs function can have significant impact on the site, as well, as overall visitor and traffic performance.

__ Short and memorable
__ Uses Keywords
__ Used in email addresses
__ Uses Favicon
__ Site.com redirect to www. version:
__ Alternate Domain redirects
__ Home page redirect to root
__ No underscores in filenames
__ Keywords in directory names
__ Multiple pages per directory
__ Registered for 5+ years
__ Multiple versions:

- .com
- .org
- .net
- .biz

__ Hyphenations
__ Misspellings
__ Product names
__ Brand names
__ Type-in keywords URLs

Site Logo

Why this is important: The logo lends directly to brand identity and site identification.

It also creates a certain element of appeal and professionalism in the mind of the visitor. It holds an important role in visitor assurance and navigation.

__ Displays company name clearly
__ Isn't hidden among clutter
__ Links to home page
__ Unique and original
__ Use tagline consistently across site

Design Considerations

Why this is important: The site design is essentially the first impression that someone gets when they land on your site. You may have all your usability and SEO elements in place, but if the design is lacking then your visitor's impression of you will be lacking, as well. A visually appealing site can not only bolster trust and credibility, but it can make you stand out among other less-appealing sites in your industry.

__ Instant site identification
__ Crisp, clean image quality
__ Clean, clutter-less design
__ Consistent colors and type
__ Whitespace usage
__ Minimal distractions
__ Targets intended audience
__ Meets industry best practices
__ Easy to navigate
__ Descriptive links
__ Good on-page organization
__ Easy to find phone number
__ Don't link screen captures
__ Skip option for flash
__ Consistent page formatting
__ No/minimal on-page styling
__ Avoid text in images
__ Font size is adequate
__ Font type is friendly
__ Paragraphs not too wide
__ Visual cues to important elements
__ Good overall contrast
__ Low usage of animated graphics
__ Uses obvious action objects

__ Avoid requiring plugins

__ Minimize the use of graphics

__ Understandable graphic file names

__ No horizontal scrolling

__ Non-busy background

__ Recognizable look and feel

__ Proper image / text padding

__ Uses trust symbols

__ Works on variety of resolutions

__ Works on variety of screen widths

Architectural Issues

Why this is important: Website architecture can make or break the performance of a website in the search engines. Poor architectural implementation can create numerous stumbling blocks, if not outright roadblocks, to the search engines as they attempt to crawl your website. On the other hand, a well-implemented foundation can assist both visitors and search engines as they navigate through your website, therefore increasing your site's overall performance.

__ Correct robots.txt file

__ Declare doctype in HTML

__ Validate HTML

__ Don't use frames

__ Alt tag usage on images

__ Custom 404 error page

__ Printer friendly

__ Underlined links

__ Differing link text color

__ Breadcrumb usage

__ Nofollow cart links

__ Robots.txt non-user pages

__ Nofollow non-important links

__ Review noindex usage

__ Validate CSS

__ Check broken links

__ No graphics for ON/YES, etc.

__ Page size less than 50K

__ Flat directory structure

__ Proper site hierarchy

__ Unique titles on all pages

__ Title reflects page info and heading

__ Unique descriptions on pages

__ No long-tail page descriptions

__ Proper bulleted list formats

__ Branded titles

__ No code bloat

__ Minimal use of tables

__ Nav uses absolute links

__ Good anchor text

__ Text can be resized

__ Key concepts are emphasized

__ CSS less browsing

__ Image-less browsing

__ Summarize all tables

Navigation

Why this is important: A strong, user-friendly and search engine friendly navigation is essential in helping people and bots through your site. Your visitors need to find information quickly with minimal hunting and the search engines need to be able to follow the navigation to reach all site pages with the fewest number of jumps (clicks) necessary. If the navigation is broken or doesn't get your prospective clients (or search engines) where they need to go, the performance of a site will suffer.

__ Located top or top-left
__ Consistent throughout site
__ Links to Home page
__ Links to Contact Us page
__ Links to About Us page
__ Simple to use
__ Indicates current page
__ Links to all main sections
__ Proper categorical divisions
__ Non-clickable is obvious
__ Accurate description text
__ Links to Login
__ Provides Logout link
__ Uses Alt attribute in images
__ No pop-up windows
__ No new window links
__ Do not rely on rollovers
__ Avoid cascading menus

__ Targets expert and novice users

__ Absolute links

Content

Why this is important: Content is an essential part of the persuasion process. Pretty, image-based sites may be appealing to the eye, but it's the content that appeals to the emotional and logical centers of the brain. The inclusion of content as well as the effectiveness of the writing are all crucially important to the sales process.

__ Grabs visitor attention

__ Exposes need

__ Demonstrates importance

__ Ties need to benefits

__ Justifies and calls to action

__ Gets to best stuff quickly

__ Reading level is appropriate

__ Client focused

__ Benefits and features

__ Targets personas

__ Provides reassurances

__ Consistent voice

__ Eliminate superfluous text

__ Reduce/explain industry jargon

__ No typo, spelling or grammar errors

__ Contains internal contextual links

__ Links out to authoritative sources

__ Enhancing keyword usage (SEO)

___ Date published on articles/news

___ Web version of PDF docs available

___ Consistent use of phrasing

___ No unsubstantiated statements

Content Appearance

Why this is important: Great content can get lost if it's not easy to read or thrown into an otherwise cluttered page. Ensuring that your content fits visually into the site is just as important as having good content to begin with.

___ Short paragraphs

___ Uses sub-headings

___ Uses bulleted lists

___ Calls to action on all pages

___ Good contrast

___ No overly small text for body

___ No overly small text for headings

___ Skimmable and scannable

___ Keep link options in close proximity

Links And Buttons

Why this is important: Links and calls to action are a great way to allow visitors to navigate from page to page, finding the information they feel is important to helping them make the purchase decision. Without these calls to action many visitors will simply not know what they are expected to do next.

__ Limit the number of links on a page
__ Avoid small buttons and tiny text for links
__ Leave space between links and buttons
__ Avoid using images as the only link
__ Link important commands
__ Underline all links
__ Accurately reflects the page it refers

Home Page

Why this is important: The home page is often the single largest entry-point. It is the page that gives the visitor the sense of who you are and what they can expect. Go wrong here and it can be all over before it begins.

__ No splash page
__ Instant page identification
__ No Flash
__ Provides overview of site
__ Site purpose is clear
__ Robot meta: NOODP, NOYDIR

About Us Page

Why this is important: Studies have shown that conversion rates for visitors who have visited the About Us page increase measurably. Those who visit here are looking for a few extra elements of trust that will help them decide whether to continue on or move on. What they find can mean the difference in a conversion or the visitor leaving your site for a competitor's.

__ Adequately describes company

__ Shows team biographies

__ Shows mission statement

__ Up to date information

__ Note associations, certifications and awards

__ Links to support pages:

__ Contact page

__ Investor relations

__ Company news

__ Registration info

__ Job opportunities

__ Newsletters

__ Link to social media profiles

Contact Us Page

Why this is important: Those who land on this page are showing clear intent in wanting to to get in touch with you. Providing only a few ways to contact you can alienate visitors who have a particular preference. Providing robust contact options and information ensures that you capture as many would-be clients as possible.

__ Easy to find

__ Multiple contact options:

__ Phone

__ Fax

__ Email

__ Form

__ Chat

__ Client feedback

__ Street map

__ Hours of operation

__ Final call to action

__ Multiple points of contact:

__ Client service

__ Tech support

__ Inquiries

__ General info

__ Job applications

__ Billing

__ Management team

__ Ad-free

__ Form requires only essential info

Practice Area Pages

Why this is important: The services page has a very singular focus. Its job is to provide the visitor with the information about the service they need to be convinced that it is exactly what they are looking for. If your practice pages cannot convince visitors to call, then you're simply dead in the water.

__ Visible calls to action

__ Clear contact info (phone #)

__ Consistent layout

__ Clear practice presentation

__ Client reviews

___ Clutter-free page

___ Practice Areas

Help And FAQ Pages

Why this is important: If your clients are digging through your help and FAQ pages, chances are they are close to making a decision to choose your law firm and they just need a little extra bump.

___ Avoid marketing hype

___ Link to additional resources:

___ Client support

___ Q & A

Privacy And Security Pages

Why this is important: While most visitors won't read Privacy and Security pages, they do provide necessary assurances that visitors look for in terms of being able to trust you. However, when visitors do click into these pages need certain information needs to be presented to them to ensure their needs are met.

___ Present info in easy to read format

___ Provide section summaries

___ Identify information types collected

___ Explain how cookies are used

___ Explain how user information will be used

___ Explain how info will be protected

___ Link to these pages in footer

___ Provide links to contact info

Site Map

Why this is important: Site maps provide a one-click path to any destination within the site and a way for the search engines to quickly find and index all site pages. Ensuring that your site maps function properly is an important part in ensuring your visitors can find what they want quickly and all site pages get properly indexed.

__ Keep information current

__ Link to site map in footer

__ Linked from help and 404 pages

__ Provide overview paragraph

__ Provide intro to main sections

__ Visible site hierarchy

__ Descriptive text and links

__ Link to xml sitemap in robots.txt file

YOUR COMPLETE INTERNET MARKETING CHECKLIST

Checklist for off-page search engine optimization

Setup Your Company Website:

____ Build out a page on your site for each of the practice areas that you offer combined with your primary city and the sub cities that you operate

____ Optimize the website from an SEO perspective

____ Update the Title Tag on each page (Your City + [Niche Keyword]) etc.

____ Update the H1 Tag on each page to re-emphasize the keyword for that specific page

____ Validate your HTML code so it is "spider" compliant (http://validator.w3.org/)

____ Text link navigation at the bottom of the page. Use your keywords as anchor text.

____ Your description tag needs to work hand-in-hand with the Title to get the searcher to "click" on the listing

____ Every page should have a unique (60% of the words completely original) Title & Description

____ Add ALT tags to your main graphics and do not

attempt to fool the Search Engines here Place your keyword phrase in the following areas:

___ Title Tag

___ Meta Description

___ H1 tag to begin the content

___ First paragraph of content

___ Appearing in Bold or Italic in the first three paragraphs of content (if possible, not that big of a deal)

___ Appearing in the filename (or directory name)

___ Used in anchor text to either an internal page or relevant external site.

___ Fix bad links and create XML Sitemap and submit to Google and Bing

___ Install Google Analytics for Tracking

Claim Your Local Listings on:

___ Google

___ Yahoo

___ Bing

___ City Search

___ Avvo

___ Kudzu

___ Best of the Web

___ Yelp

Setup Your Social Media Profiles:

___ Facebook

___ Twitter

___ YouTube

___ Google Plus

___ LinkedIn

___ SlideShare

Post to your blog at least once per week with some tip or industry information:

___ Take that post and syndicate it online directory sites with appropriate link / anchor text pointing back to your site

___ Post to your Social Media Profiles at least 2x per day with some tip of company info

___ Add at least 2 citations per week

___ Add at least 2 inbound links per week

NEXT STEPS

Through the course of this guide, we have covered a lot of information and taken you step-by-step through the process of marketing your law firm online by optimizing your website from an SEO perspective, How to Optimize Your Website for the Most Commonly Searched law firm Keywords in your area & How to Leverage Social Media to get more repeat & referral business. If you have taken action and followed our instructions, you should be well on your way to dominating the Search Engines for the lawyer related keywords in your area.

NEED MORE HELP?

If you've gotten to this point and feel like you need some extra help to implement some of these ideas, we are here to support you. As experts in internet marketing and helping law firms, we have had tremendous success implementing these strategies. You can call us directly at 866-563-6134 with any questions that you might have or request an online marketing evaluation.

Our team will review your online marketing effort (Website, Competition, Search Engine Placement, Social Media, etc.) and come back to you with a simple video assessment of where you can improve and what you can do to take your online marketing efforts to the next level.

Why would you work with us? The reason is simple. We know that once you see that...we're genuinely interested in working with you to get real results for your law firm...and when you see the ideas and strategies we suggest based around YOUR law firm and what you want from your business...we know there's a very good chance you'll hire us or introduce us to another lawyer or law firm you think we can help. Plus, we offer a double money back guarantee.

5 Things that Set Us Apart from the Industry

1. We do not piece meal your work out. We do all the work from your website to SEO, video production and marketing, tracking and even pitching producers.

2. We are not attorneys. We are not carrying a caseload and working on your marketing part-time. We are a full-time marketing agency focused in the legal industry.

3. I am the expert. I understand how marketing works from video marketing, social media, content development and marketing. I don't talk the talk like most agencies do I have the results to back it up.

4. We work exclusively with you. We only work with one lawyer per practice area per city. Our goal is to help you dominate.

5. We only work with lawyers and law firms. We understand that there are certain guidelines that we must follow for lawyers from the policies, handbooks and social media posts. We market effectively for your firm.

Either way you get the complete assessment and a whole pile of ideas and suggestions that you can implement right away. Our time is limited and we can only offer a few of these consultations each month.

If you'd like to take advantage of this unique chance to talk to an Internet Marketing professional then... call us directly at 866-563-6134 or request your online marketing evaluation.

Request A Free Custom Online Marketing Evaluation Now.
http://www.HowToMarketYourLawFirmOnline.com/

SERVICES

Our goal will be to help our client obtain top page placement on Google, Yahoo & Bing in the Organic (non Pay-Per-Click) section of the Search Engines for the most important Keywords in and around their Area.

- SEO – We will build a new / updated version of the website on their existing domain (or a new one if necessary) and build out and further optimize for the Important Related Terms in their Area

- Video Marketing – We are going to create a 26 or 52-week content marketing strategy with our full service video production and marketing services that showcase your business. We will shoot original footage on location with expert lighting and sound to convey a professional image to your future clients. We will also optimize your new videos for maximum exposure on social media platforms and your website.

- Link Building & Content Development - Once the On Page SEO work is complete, the only way to get your site to rise above the competition is by building quality inbound links. We will systematically develop inbound links from quality sources on your behalf via Competitive Link Acquisition, Article Distribution, Video Distribution, Social Media Bookmarking and a variety of other sources.

- Map Listing & Directory Optimization – Our team will Claim, Optimize & Building Out your map and directory listings on popular map / directory sites such as Google Places (AKA Google Map Listing), Bing Local Listing, Yahoo Local Listing, Yelp, CitySearch, Avvo, and many other local directories.

- Social Media Marketing – We will leverage your existing Social Media Profiles on Facebook, Twitter, Google Plus, & YouTube. As part of this service our team will be consistently posting to the major social media sites on your behalf on a daily basis. The majority of the posts will be informational in nature. E.G. How to Pick a Lawyer in Your City or What to Expect at Your First Attorney Consultation

- Newsletter and Direct Mail Marketing - We will prepare a monthly or quarterly newsletter or sales letter for up to 100 clients per month. We will create all of the content, ship the newsletters and provide feedback.

- ReTargeting – Low Hanging Fruit. We will add a pixel to your website so that we can market to your prospects even after they leave your site.

- Reputation Marketing - The key to getting the most from your online marketing & social media efforts is to have an automated marketing follow up system in place. We will be equipping you to collect contact information from your clients (name, email address & mobile number) and then systematically follow up with them for maximum effect:

- Authority Building through Video - Set-up and optimize your YouTube channel, research top video keywords, Submit People on the Move, Generate Press Release, Submit 4 videos to YouTube, Create YouTube Channel Trailer,

- Track, Measure & Quantify - To help you measure the results of our efforts and quantity your Return On Investment you will get the following reports on an ongoing Basis:

Traffic & Search Trends - We will install Google Analytics on your site so that you can see exactly how many people are hitting your site on a monthly basis, what words they typed in to get to the site, what pages they visited, etc. You will receive this report on a monthly basis via eMail.

SEO Page Placement Report - We will setup a report with the Core Keywords that we are looking to obtain placement for and systematically track that placement on Google, Yahoo, & Bing. You will receive a weekly status update report indicating your page placement for each of your keywords.

Call Tracking - We will provide you with unique tracking numbers for each of your locations. With these numbers in place we will be able to determine exactly how many inbound calls are coming in on a monthly basis and even listen to recordings of those inbound calls.

Additional Considerations:

- We provide all the services listed above for a term commitment – 6 or 12 months

- Everything that we do for you is YOURS TO KEEP. All of the pages that we develop, content we write and links we acquire on your behalf are yours for the keeping even if you decide to stop working with us.

- Number of Cities - Our program includes optimization for your Primary Practice and City.

- Number of Google Places Listings - Our program assumes 1 primary Google Places Listing / Location.

- We offer exclusivity and only work with 1 law firm in 1 practice area in 1 city.

- 180 day money back guarantee*

We would only be working with one law firm with one area of practice in your city. This is on a first come first serve basis. Your competitor may have downloaded this guide too. So if this sounds of interest to you give me a call right away before one of your competitors hires us and we won't be able to work with you anyways. If you'd like to take advantage of this unique chance to talk to an Internet Marketing professional then... call us directly at 866-563-6134 or request your online marketing evaluation.

Request A Free Custom Online Marketing Evaluation Now.
http://www.HowToMarketYourLawFirmOnline.com

AUTHOR BIO

Montina Portis is the CEO of the CIA, Creative Internet Authority, a full service law firm marketing agency specializing in lead conversion for boutique and small size law firms. Over 20,000 clients have benefited from learning and implementing the proven marketing strategies taught by Montina. Through various online marketing tools including video and social media she helps lawyers establish a leading brand presence, automate marketing and enhance their reputations online.

With a strong blend of education, technology and marketing with her 15 years in the business world, Montina is focused on targeted and efficient results. She is a column contributor with Above the Law.

She works exclusively with lawyers and law firms to attract new clients, generate more referrals and make more money using online and offline legal marketing strategies. Through various online marketing tools including video and social media she helps lawyers establish a leading brand presence, automate marketing and enhance their reputation online.

Find out more about Montina at www.MontinaPortis.com

FAQs

1. What if I want more than one market area eventually?

We would set up another plan for you. Same price because we work with you exclusively.

2. Who writes all of the posts and articles?

We have 2 content writers that we recently hired full-time to write the blog posts and articles. Our social media manager works with them to pull the content from the blog posts and articles to post on your social media profiles. We focus only on legal marketing so that we can make sure that we are abiding by best practices for each state. Unlike most companies we work exclusively in your industry and will not work with competitors in your city. For instance in Georgia we abide by the Georgia State Bar Rules 7.1-7.5 that discuss communications and advertising. http://www.gabar.org/barrules/handbookdetail.cfm?what=rule&id=145

4.   Is your web developer local or based out of another country?

Based out of another country. He has been a part of my team for 2 years'.

5.   How much time should/would I expect to spend preparing for the videos?

3-4 hours the day of the shoot and at least 1-2 hours after we initially send them. These are questions you would already be familiar with and we will meet via phone before the day of the shoot to answer any questions you may have.

6.   How often will you post content on my social media pages?

Daily on weekdays

7.   I'm not in Savannah, Georgia. I would want a different location. Confirm location availability.

Before we schedule a meeting with you we will let you know if we have your practice area and city available.

8.   How do you go about collecting the customer/client reviews?

We use multiple systems depending on each client one of which includes - http://birdeye.com

9.   My understanding, based on our call, was the your web designer would re-design the website to make it more productive. The proposal seems to indicate otherwise (i.e., that you will work with my web designer). Please clarify.

If you have a web designer we would work with them. If not, our web designer would re-design the website.

10. Tell me more about the video Q&A days and how that works.

Before your video shoot we develop questions from our keyword research, lawyer.com and your practice area and send them to you at least 3 weeks before your scheduled shoot. We then have a 30 minute conference call to review the questions and discuss the videos.

On the day of the shoot you can expect a professional videographer and at times a photographer along with me in attendance. I will direct the videos and make sure that the content is consistent and your energy stays high during the shoot.

We suggest that you bring along a change of clothes and work with you and have guidelines we send out beforehand that outlines what to wear, etc.

I will then direct you and you will record 1-3 minute videos based on the topics we have chosen. We then take these videos and distribute them online. We ask that you set aside up to 4 hours so that we can record at least 25 - 40 videos to distribute online. Although this is only 75 - 120 minutes we find that most clients do not make it through each video without making a few mistakes.

11. Why is video marketing important?

The future of Internet is video. Video is amazing for SEO because from one video we can syndicate it for social media posts, audios, blog posts and simple FAQs and build an educational library for your site.

Video marketing has a huge affect on sales:

- Online video users are expected to double to 1.5 billion in 2016.

- Globally, online video traffic will be 55 percent of all consumer Internet traffic in 2016.

- 76 percent of marketers plan to add video to their sites, making it a higher priority than Facebook, Twitter and blog integration.

- More than 1 billion unique users visit YouTube each month, spending more than 4 billion hours watching videos.

- 2 billion video views per week are monetized on YouTube, and every auto-shared tweet results in six new YouTube browsing sessions. (Digiday)

12. How does the video marketing for referrals work? Are links sent to current clients?

Using one of our reputation systems we request reviews from your current clients. On the day of the video shoot we would want you to create a video thanking your clients for their business and requesting referrals.

Once they provide a review we follow-up with a thank you video. We also take your current reviews and can create videos from them to market your reputation online.

LEGAL TRADE ASSOCIATIONS

American Bankruptcy Institute (ABI)

The largest multi-disciplinary, non-partisan initiative of its kind, ABI dedicates its energies to research and public education on bankruptcy and related issues. Established in 1982, its membership roll lists more than 11,000 lawyers, bankers, judges, lenders, academicians and other professionals in the field.

www.abiworld.org

American Bar Association

The American Bar Association is the largest voluntary professional organization worldwide. Consisting of 400,000 members, the ABA offers education, information and programs to attorneys, judges, the business community and the general public. One of its most critical functions is the accreditation of law schools.

www.abanet.org

American Immigration Lawyers Association

Affiliated with the American Bar Association, AILA offers members legal and professional education and services through its 36 chapters and more than 50 national committees. The organization's membership boasts over 10,000 attorneys and law professors who practice and teach immigration law, representing thousands of families seeking permanent residence in the U.S. The AILA likewise aids foreign students, entertainers, athletes and individuals seeking asylum, as well as U.S. businesses that employ highly skilled foreign workers.

www.aila.org

Commercial Law League of America

With a membership of more than 4,000 legal and financial professionals, the CLLA advocates in the both commercial law and bankruptcy disciplines, representing both creditor interests and businesses and individuals experiencing fiscal difficulties. The organization formed in 1895, making it one of the oldest and most respected of its genre.

www.clla.org

American Intellectual Property Law Association

The American Intellectual Property Law Association (AIPLA) is a national bar association constituted primarily of lawyers in private and corporate practice, in government service, and in the academic community, with approximately 15,000 members. AIPLA represents a wide and diverse spectrum of individuals from law firms, companies, and institutions involved directly or indirectly in the practice of patent, trademark, copyright, and unfair competition law, as well as other fields of law affecting intellectual property. Our members represent both owners and users of intellectual property.

www.aipla.org

American Law Institute

The American Law Institute is the leading independent organization in the United States producing scholarly work to clarify, modernize, and otherwise improve the law. The Institute (made up of 4000 lawyers, judges, and law professors of the highest qualifications) drafts, discusses, revises, and publishes Restatements of the Law, model statutes, and principles of law that are enormously influential in the courts and legislatures, as well as in legal scholarship and education. ALI has long been influential internationally and, in recent years, more of its work has become international in scope.

www.ali.org

American Association For Justice

The Mission of the American Association for Justice is to promote a fair and effective justice system—and to support the work of attorneys in their efforts to ensure that any person who is injured by the misconduct or negligence of others can obtain justice in America's courtrooms, even when taking on the most powerful interests.

Formerly the Association of Trial Lawyers of America

www.atlanet.org

American Academy of Estate Planning Attorneys

The American Academy of Estate Planning Attorneys is the premier national organization promoting excellence in estate planning by providing its exclusive membership of attorneys with up-to-date research, educational materials, and other vital practice management techniques. You don't have to take our word for it, the Academy has been recognized by Money Magazine, The John Tesh Radio Show and Suze Orman in her book, 9 Steps to Financial Freedom.

www.aaepa.com

American Civil Liberties Union

For nearly 100 years, the ACLU has been our nation's guardian of liberty, working in courts, legislatures, and communities to defend and preserve the individual rights and liberties that the Constitution and the laws of the United States guarantee everyone in this country.

Whether it's achieving full equality for lesbians, gays, bisexuals and transgender people; establishing new privacy protections for our digital age of widespread government surveillance; ending mass incarceration; or preserving the right to vote or the right to have an abortion; the ACLU takes up the toughest civil liberties cases and issues to defend all people from government abuse and overreach.

With more than a million members, activists, and supporters, the ACLU is a nationwide organization that fights tirelessly in all 50 states, Puerto Rico, and Washington, D.C. to safeguard everyone's rights.

www.aclu.org

American Association of Law Libraries

The American Association of Law Libraries was founded in 1906 to promote and enhance the value of law libraries to the legal and public communities, to foster the profession of law librarianship, and to provide leadership in the field of legal information.

Today, with nearly 5,000 members, the Association represents law librarians and related professionals who are affiliated with a wide range of institutions: law firms; law schools; corporate legal departments; courts; and local, state, and federal government agencies.

The American Association of Law Libraries advances the profession of law librarianship and supports the professional growth of its members through leadership and advocacy in the field of legal information and information policy.

www.aallnet.org

American Society For Pharmacy Law

The American Society for Pharmacy Law (ASPL) is the organization of attorneys, pharmacists, pharmacist-attorneys and students of pharmacy or law who are interested in the law as it applies to pharmacy, pharmacists, wholesalers, manufacturers, state and federal government and other interested parties.

www.aspl.org

American Society of International Law

The mission of the American Society of International Law (ASIL) is to foster the study of international law and to promote the establishment and maintenance of international relations on the basis of law and justice.

www.asil.org

American Tort Reform Association (ATRA)

ATRA is the only national organization exclusively dedicated to repairing our civil justice system. ATRA fights in Congress, in state legislatures, and in the courts to make the system fairer.

www.atra.org

Association of Attorney-mediators

The Association of Attorney-Mediators ("AAM") was originally founded by the late Steve Brutsché in 1989, and incorporated as a non-profit in 1991. AAM's creation was the result of the inception of mediation by professional attorney-mediators in Texas, where the first two areas to embrace the process were Dallas and Houston.

www.attorney-mediators.org

Black Entertainment & Sports Lawyers Association

BESLA (Black Entertainment and Sports Lawyers Association) is a nationally recognized leader in legal education and professional development within the United States for lawyers and professionals in the entertainment, sports, and related industries.

www.besla.org

Education Law Association

The Education Law Association (ELA) is a national, nonprofit member association offering unbiased information to its professional members about current legal issues affecting education and the rights of those involved in education in bothe public and private K - 12 schools, universities, and colleges.

www.educationlaw.org

Environmental Law Institute

The Environmental Law Institute (ELI) makes law work for people, places, and the planet. ELI's Vision is "a healthy environment, prosperous economies, and vibrant communities founded on the rule of law."

www2.eli.org

International Technology Law Association

ITechLaw has been serving the technology law community worldwide since 1971 and is one of the most widely established and largest associations of its kind. It has a global membership base representing six continents and spanning more than 60 countries. Its members and officials reflect a broad spectrum of expertise in the technology law field.

www.itechlaw.org

National Association of Consumer Bankruptcy Attorneys

NACBA is the only national organization dedicated to serving the needs of consumer bankruptcy attorneys and protecting the rights of consumer debtors in bankruptcy. Formed in 1992, NACBA now has more than 4,000 members located in all 50 states and Puerto Rico.

www.nacba.org

National Association of Criminal Lawyers

The National Association of Criminal Defense Lawyers (NACDL) encourages, at all levels of federal, state and local government, a rational and humane criminal justice policy for America -- one that promotes fairness for all; due process for even the least among us who may be accused of wrongdoing; compassion for witnesses and victims of crime; and just punishment for the guilty.

www.criminaljustice.org

National Association of Patent Practitioners

The National Association of Patent Practitioners (NAPP) is a nonprofit organization dedicated to supporting patent practitioners and those working in the field of patent law in matters relating to patent prosecution, its practice, and technological advances.

www.napp.org

National Employment Lawyers Association

The National Employment Lawyers Association (NELA) advances employee rights and serves lawyers who advocate for equality and justice in the American workplace.

NELA is the country's largest professional organization that is exclusively comprised of lawyers who represent individual employees in cases involving employment discrimination and other employment-related matters.

www.nela.org

National Lawyers Guild

The NLG is dedicated to the need for basic change in the structure of our political and economic system.

www.nlg.org